Introduction to
BATIK

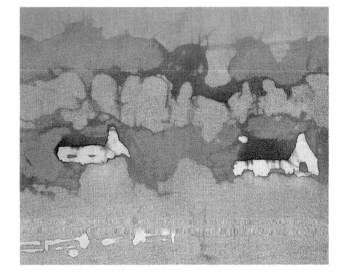

Introduction to batik

Batik is a very ancient craft dating back at least two thousand years. It can be defined as a method of applying a coloured design on to textiles by waxing those parts that are not to be dyed. Evidence of its practice has been discovered in most Eastern and Middle Eastern countries including India, China, Japan, Persia and Egypt, but although its actual source is unknown, it was on the island of Java in Indonesia that the art reached its peak of development. Through the centuries Javanese craftsmen have perfected the art, reflecting the culture and religion of their country in the richness of colours and the detail of the designs on their fabrics. These traditional designs have been passed on from one generation to another and are mainly based on the flora and fauna of their surroundings and this form of expression adapts to society now as easily as it did so many years ago.

Batik has evolved around the principle that wax and water repel each other, therefore an area of fabric that has been covered with wax is unable to accept dye. The Indonesian word 'tik', meaning a drop (referring to the small drops of hot wax), shows how the word 'batik' was derived. It is an exciting medium for beginners to explore because there is always an element of surprise when the wax is removed from the fabric and the hidden effect is revealed. Careful waxing should ensure that the surprise is a pleasant one and not the reverse! The effect one colour has on another is particularly exciting, even to the more experienced batik artist. With adequate supervision, children enjoy experimenting with batik. They talk to us at craft fairs about their work and show a great deal of interest in our designs.

White pure cotton, (or white pure silk), is the best material to use for batik. Hot wax is applied to the fabric in the areas that are to be kept white and then the dye is added. The lightest colour is the first dye. The fabric is then waxed in those areas that are to be kept in this first colour and the process repeated with a second colour. Waxing and dyeing in this way is continued until the desired effect is achieved; the last and darkest colour being black. Since colours are merging during the dyeing process, in unwaxed areas, it is important to adhere to a particular colour scale. For example, if the first dye is red and the second blue, keep in mind that the result is not blue but violet. Once all the dyeing is complete, the wax is then removed revealing the design.

Fine cracks can occur in the wax during the process, or can be deliberately planned as part of the design. When the wax cracks, the dye penetrates the fabric in these places and gives the batik its distinctive veined look, though some artists prefer to have little or no cracking at all.

Every batik is a one-off original. You may, of course, attempt to reproduce a previously successful design, but it will always have an originality of its own because of the nature of the craft. It is impossible to duplicate exactly the application, or the random crackle pattern of the wax, or even guarantee the precise colour values. Your personal approach to this exciting medium will ensure that you develop your own particular style and understanding of the potential of batik.

The Hollyford Track by Heather Griffin
Wax and several different coloured dyes are applied to white cotton, before the waxed fabric is cracked and dipped in dark green dye, giving the effect of trees and foliage. Further waxing and dyeing creates the darker tree trunks and shadows. For detailed instructions on how to make the picture opposite, see pages 46 and 47.

Uses for batik fabrics

In any area of design where a fabric is the main constituent, batik can play an exciting part in the decoration. We have shown a variety of designs on the following pages, including coats, blouses, tops, bows, scarves, a wall hanging and picture; there are many more applications for this craft and a few are listed below.

Clothes: there is a great deal of satisfaction to be gained by wearing clothes made from your own original batik design. The simplest clothes can easily be made by you if you wish, but it is also possible to buy ready made white cotton and silk garments and set about creating your own batik design on them. Children's clothes look particularly attractive.

If you want to make your own clothes, there are several ways of applying a batik design.

1. Retain the material in one piece with the shapes of the pattern pieces lightly drawn on, thus enabling you to see where your batik design will be on the finished garment.
2. Having several smaller pieces of material (not cut to pattern).
3. Having material cut to pattern but on a slightly larger scale than the finished pattern pieces, to allow for a certain amount of fraying at the edges, or slight shrinkage. The batik pieces are then finally cut to the correct size.

Scarves: this is a very attractive method of using batik, especially in silk. Scarves can also be bought ready made in white silk or you can, of course, make your own in either silk or cotton (see opposite and page 28).

Belts and hair bows: these simple items make original personal or bazaar gifts, (see pages 26 and 27 for bows).

Wallhangings: these can be quite basic, with very few colours, through to complicated pictures requiring much creative planning.

Soft furnishings: batik may be used for many household purposes such as blinds, curtains, cushion covers, lampshades, tablecloths, bedspreads, all designed to complement your own colour schemes.

Mirror and picture frames: this is a most original way of adding a personal touch to ordinary household items.

Greetings cards: if you are reluctant to tackle a large area of fabric, begin by experimenting with a small remnant which can be mounted as a personal greetings card.

Soft toys: these can allow you to give full rein to your imagination. Tigers and tabby cats lend themselves particularly well to this application of the craft.

Perhaps you can think of other applications for a textile which features your own unique design.

Silk scarf designs by Margaret Hone
A luxurious, beautifully coloured silk scarf is the perfect gift or accessory. Simple designs can be applied to bought scarves, or hand-made scarves can be created from odd pieces of silk, and one or two dyes applied.
The central blue and white scarf is coloured with just one dye. It is worked flat on a sheet of greaseproof paper and an abstract design drawn straight on to the fabric with wax, leaving larger areas free to take the dye. It is then dipped in blue dye and when dry the wax is removed (see page 19 for instructions on removing wax from silk).
When using two or more dyes, follow the method shown on pages 21–25. More detailed instructions for applying batik to scarves are found on page 28.

Design sources

Ideas for batik designs are everywhere. If you are already an accomplished artist you will probably have your own sources of ideas and sketches to work from, but a beginner in batik can just as easily find inspiration.

Before beginning, you must decide what you are going to make and then consider the most suitable type of design. This could be abstract, representational or geometric. Always bear in mind the measurements of your material against the scale of your design.

It is not necessary to be a superb artist to create a good design. A simple composition, just based on random blocks of colour, can be very successful. Inspiration for design can be drawn from many sources; nature, photographs, postcards, text books, paintings, magazines, posters, greetings cards and everyday objects.

Nature is a never ending source of inspiration. So are household pets and the plants, flowers and trees in your garden. Fruits and vegetables, when cut open, give unusual abstract designs, as do patterns made by clouds, waves and rock formations. A camera is invaluable for instantly recording something that catches your eye, or you can make sketches with detailed colour notes.

As colour is such an essential part of batik, it is a most important feature of the design and must be carefully planned in advance.

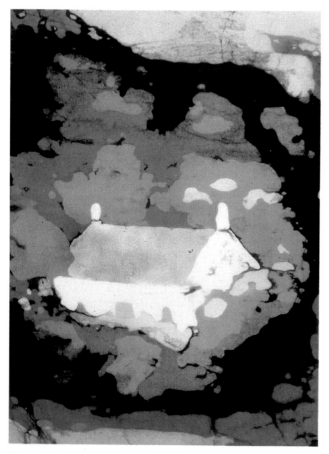

Sailboard and landscape designs by Heather Griffin
The two contrasting pictures on this page show details taken from batik shirts. They illustrate effectively how ideas for design can be found almost anywhere. For detailed instructions in how to create these designs, see pages 39–41.

Equipment and materials

Before you can begin any batik project, make sure that you have all the necessary equipment and materials available. They are as follows:

Fabric
Wooden frames
Drawing pins, safety pins, dressmaking pins or masking tape
Soft pencil, for drawing or tracing the design on to the fabric
Wax
Wax pot or a double saucepan
Brushes
Tjantings
Dye bath
Cold water dyes and fixing agents as recommended by the manufacturers
Large saucepan or metal bucket
Plastic buckets
Wooden tongs
Cleaning solvent
Rubber gloves
Plastic apron
Plastic clothes pegs
Teaspoons
Jam jars
Newspapers, greaseproof paper
Tracing paper
Paper tissues or kitchen roll

Fabrics

These must be manufactured from natural fibres, such as pure cotton, linen, muslin, poplin, silk and satin. It is best to wash all fabrics before beginning to work on them, to remove any dressing that may effect the penetration of the dyes. Cotton can be boiled if necessary. Synthetic fabrics are not suitable as they do not hold the dye satisfactorily.

Wooden frames

The fabric has to be stretched over a wooden frame before applying the hot wax. Ready made, adjustable batik frames can be purchased from craft shops. These are excellent, but expensive. Alternatively oil painting stretcher frames can be used. These come in a variety of sizes and the soft wood facilitates the use of drawing pins. Old picture frames can also be used, but they are often made from harder wood. You can, of course, make up your own simple wooden frame.

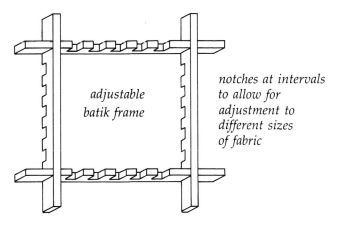

adjustable batik frame

notches at intervals to allow for adjustment to different sizes of fabric

It is a good idea to have one frame bound with strips of old sheeting and plastic, to be kept for use with silk and fine fabrics so the material can be attached to the frame with dressmakers' pins. If the silk is very fine it can be attached to the frame with masking tape or alternatively you could work without a frame. The silk should be laid out on a flat surface over a sheet of greaseproof paper before applying the wax.

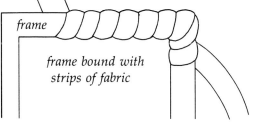

frame

frame bound with strips of fabric

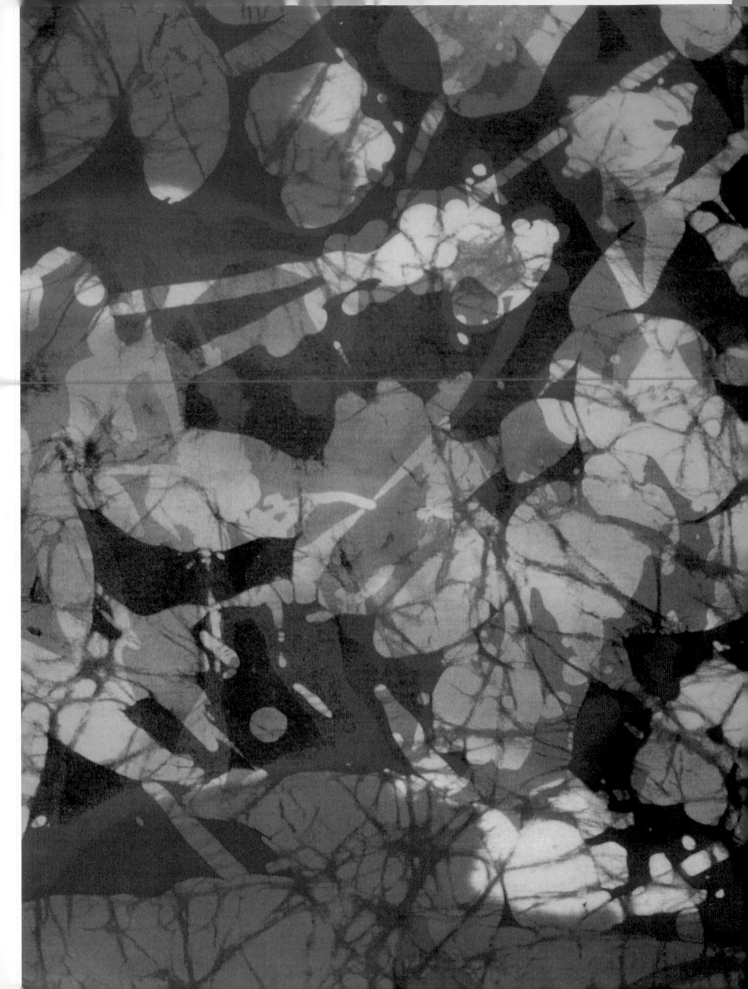

out of the reservoir, leaving only enough to run freely from the spout. This technique is not easy and it requires practice and patience to perfect.

Check the back of the batik from time to time to ensure that all areas have been penetrated by the wax. If not, turn the fabric over and rewax the back of the material where necessary. Mistakes made at this stage are not easy to correct, for once the wax is applied to the fabric it is difficult to remove, although not impossible.

Waxing double thicknesses of cotton

It is possible to wax through double thicknesses of cotton and silk, when you wish to have an identical design on both sides. On an item or garment that is already made up this is obviously a useful way to work.

Ensure that the double material is pulled taut on the frame. When waxing, force the hot wax through both thicknesses of cloth. Keep checking the underside of the material and re-wax if necessary.

Proceed with the dyeing and waxing as usual, taking care not to separate the two pieces of fabric until you reach the final stage of removing the wax.

If you do not wish to carry a design through to the back of a ready-made item, it is possible to separate the back and front by inserting greaseproof paper between the thicknesses.

Mistakes in waxing

To remove an unwanted area of wax, scrape as much wax as possible from both sides of the fabric with a knife. Then rub the area with a metal teaspoon that has been immersed in boiling water. Repeat the treatment until all the wax has been removed. The fabric must be completely free of wax before the dye can penetrate.

If, during the waxing process, the temperature of the wax has cooled giving an area of opaque wax, remove this carefully with a knife and re-wax.

Dyeing

We use the same dyes for silk as for cotton but the biggest difference is in the depth and tone of the colour. On silk the same solution of dye is sometimes several shades lighter than on cotton. Therefore, if you want to obtain deeper shades, you have to mix a stronger dye solution. There are special dyes available for use on silk only.

Now you are ready for the first dye. Mix your chosen colour with the fixatives as instructed by the manufacturer and pour the dye into a dye bath, first checking that it has been thoroughly mixed. Make sure the dye bath is large enough to allow the batik to be submerged easily and moved about.

Remember, the dyeing process always proceeds stage by stage from the lightest to the darkest colour.

Remove the cloth from the frame and, wearing rubber gloves and an apron, immerse the batik in the dye, keeping the fabric as flat as possible otherwise the wax will crack at this early stage.

If you deliberately want to introduce the fine lines that give batik its characteristic look at this early stage, just gently crumple the material before submerging it in the dye. This will 'crack' the wax, and the dye can penetrate the cloth. During the dyeing processes the dyes will automatically penetrate any cracks that may appear.

Ensure that the dye has penetrated the unwaxed fabric and remove it from the dye bath. Bear in mind that colours show up stronger on wet fabric. To get more of an idea of the shade, hold the batik up to a light or a window. If the colour is not strong enough, make a stronger mixture and submerge the

Detail from random-patterned waistcoat by Margaret Hone
Different colours are mixed and randomly applied to white cotton, which is then waxed. A final dipping in black dye creates the lovely design shown opposite. For detailed instructions see page 37.

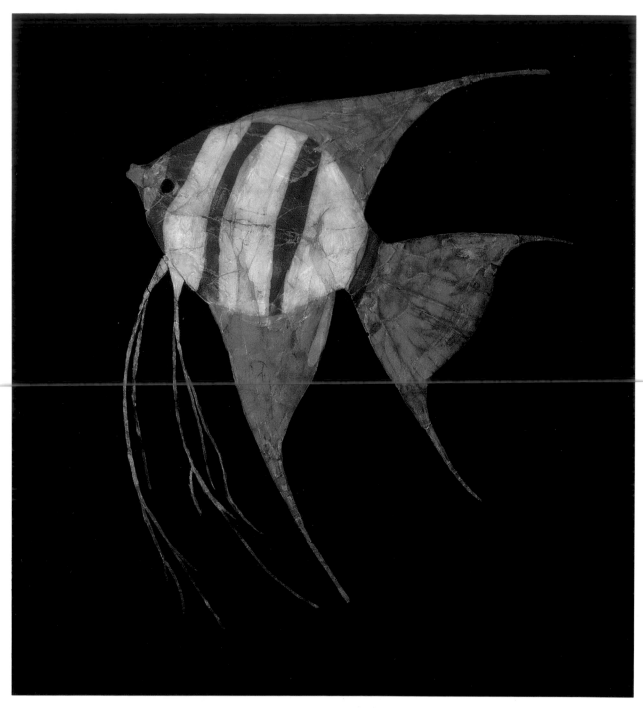

When dry, wax areas to be kept orange and lightly crack the design by gently crumpling the fabric, before dipping the batik into the final blue dye. This gives a brown background with blue cracks on the white areas, green on the yellow and brown on the orange. Leave to dry overnight and remove the wax by the boiling method.

After the wax has been removed and the batik has been allowed to dry, the colours appear much lighter. Now you can make your wallhanging.

Neaten your completed batik by trimming off approximately 2.5 cm (1 in) all round the edges.

Now hem the long side edges and make open-ended hems, at top and bottom edges. Allow enough space to insert the wooden dowelling. Insert wooden dowelling into top and bottom hems and attach a length of cord to the top edge.

Silk scarves

A silk scarf complemented with an original design is an ideal gift or accessory. These scarves were purchased already made up and the fine silk gives a delicate effect, even with quite strong dyes. It is not possible to make very strong contrasts in colours on this material, although heavier silks such as crepe de Chine, silk satin and silk twill react better to stronger dyes.

The scarves opposite demonstrate that batik on fine lightweight silk achieves rather lovely effects. They are all made by the same method. This method is explained below, taking the scarf in the top left of the picture as the example. Use the techniques described earlier in this book to create designs like the ones shown opposite.

Materials

1 purchased white Habotai silk square, 90 × 90cm (35 ½ × 35 ½ in).
Blue, red, brown dyes
Microcrystalline wax

Method

Very simple techniques are used to create this lovely scarf. Although three dyes are used, there is only one colour dipping. Small amounts of wax are used making possible the addition of several other colours by painting on. The white silk scarf is laid on greaseproof paper and using a 2.5 cm (1 in) wide brush an abstract 'starfish' design is painted on to the fabric with the melted wax.

When the wax has cooled, the scarf is laid flat in strong blue dye for a few minutes. It is then removed and laid out flat on clean, dry newspaper.

It is better to dry fine silk scarves in this way, rather than hanging them up, as there is less likelihood of damage. The newspaper absorbs the dye quickly, resulting in a lighter colour. Large sheets of plastic can be used for the same purpose, but the dye will not be absorbed and therefore a deeper colour may be obtained. When the blue dye has dried, the scarf is laid

out on greaseproof paper again for rewaxing. Some small dribbles of wax are allowed to run on to the blue silk, enclosing areas of the fabric. This will act as a barrier to the dyes used in the final process.

When the wax is cold, the scarf is laid on newspaper. Small amounts of red and brown dyes are mixed in separate jars and painted on to the scarf, filling in the spaces enclosed by wax only. Some blue areas are left unpainted. The red dye turns mauve as it mixes with the background blue, and the brown dye is used as a contrast against the lighter colours.

The scarf is left to dry overnight and the wax removed, (see page 19).

Silk scarf designs by Margaret Hone
Lovely delicate effects can be achieved by applying wax and dyes to silk. The colours and patterns on the scarves shown opposite are all created using the techniques illustrated in this book.

Silk summer top

Three dyes are used on this simple silk top to create a batik landscape in greens and blues.

Materials
Purchased pattern
White silk crepe de Chine, as required
Turquoise, yellow, royal blue dyes
Paraffin wax

Method
The silk is cut into two pieces; these are placed together and pinned with dressmakers' pins to a bound frame; then the outline of the back of the garment is drawn lightly on to the top of the silk in pencil, using the pattern as a guide.

The chosen design is pencilled on to the silk, within the pattern area, and then the wax is applied through the double thickness of silk to the areas to remain white – tree trunks, clouds, fences and cottages. It is advisable to check the back of the silk pieces before continuing, to make sure the wax has penetrated the two thicknesses. If not, turn the frame over and retouch areas that need waxing.

When the wax is cold, the silk is unpinned from the frame, keeping the two pieces together by pinning the edges – in parts they are already firmly held together by the wax, the pins are an added precaution to prevent the two pieces separating during the dyeing processes. The top is dipped in turquoise dye.

When dry, the silk is transferred to the frame and tree shapes, foliage and hedgerows waxed over the turquoise. Yellow dye is painted on to make green.

When dry, the whole area of silk is covered with wax. When it is cold, the sky and trees are deliberately cracked by crumpling the silk

Silk summer top and cropped cotton top
by Heather Griffin
A simple landscape theme gives life and colour to two white summer tops. Whether you purchase a pattern (left), or buy a garment (right), beautiful batik designs can be applied by following a few basic rules.
The picture below right shows a detail of the cropped cotton top above.

and then it is dipped into a strong royal blue dye.

The wax is removed by the hot water method, (see page 19). When the silk is dry, it is ready to be made up according to the pattern instructions. Carefully match the batik design when making up the garment.

Cropped cotton top

A purchased white cotton top is enhanced by a lovely pale summery batik landscape which is drawn on to the fabric freehand, using sketches as reference.

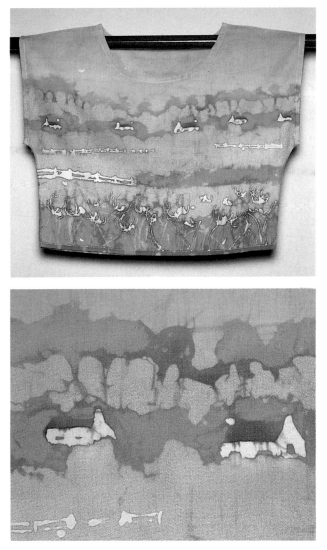

Materials

Purchased white cotton top
Pale blue, bright yellow, turquoise, red, brown, dark blue dyes
Paraffin wax

Method

The design on the back of the top is the same as the design on the front (only in reverse). So the wax is worked through the double thickness of cloth.

Before starting, a decision is made about which areas are to remain white. In this design it is the cottages (apart from the roofs), fences and the flowers in the foreground of the landscape. These areas are waxed, using a tjanting and several brushes, depending on the size of the area.

Pale blue dye is painted on to the top to represent 'sky' and yellow dye painted on to represent 'fields'. Where the two colours meet water is brushed on to blend and weaken the dye; this is then blotted with kitchen paper.

The top 'sky' section and some of the yellow 'fields' are waxed leaving areas free. These will appear as hedges, trees and grass.

The top is then dipped in turquoise blue and the 'sky' deliberately cracked by gently crumpling the fabric.

The green that results from the dipping is then kept by waxing. The cottage roofs are waxed round and when enclosed, some red and brown dyes are painted on. When dry these are waxed.

Finally, the waxed top is lightly cracked by crumpling, and then dipped in dark blue dye. Care is taken to keep the 'sky' section out of the dye bath, so that no dark cracking occurs on this area.

When dry the wax is boiled out.

Sleeveless top

The same landscape theme is used on this sleeveless top. Again the design is based on sketches and transferred to the fabric freehand.

Materials

Purchased pattern
White cotton poplin as required
Yellow, red, blue, turquoise dyes
Paraffin wax

Method

The material is cut in half and the two pieces placed together and pinned to a frame. The paper pattern and design outlines are drawn on to the material. When waxing and dyeing, carry the design out beyond the pattern lines.

Sleeveless top by Heather Griffin
The enlarged detail opposite shows the reverse side of the garment and it illustrates clearly how wax is applied to this garment to retain white areas of cotton. Cottage walls, fences and trees are waxed on to the fabric before the initial dyes are applied.

Using a tjanting and a brush, wax is applied to the areas to remain white – sky, fences, road, tree trunks and cottage walls.

Yellow dye is painted on to the material, through both thicknesses, then red dye is applied alongside the 'road'. Where the two colours merge they become orange.

The yellow areas are waxed, leaving the tree areas free. Blue dye is painted on to give a lovely leafy yellowy green. These areas are then waxed and red is painted on to the cottage roofs. When dry the roofs are waxed.

The wax covering the sky is deliberately cracked, by folding the material into horizontal lines and the whole top is removed from the frame and dipped in turquoise dye. The wax will hold the two pieces of material together, but a few dressmakers' pins attached around the edges of the fabric will ensure they will not come apart during the dyeing process.

The wax is boiled out once the material is dry. Once all the wax is removed and the material is dry, make up the pattern as directed.

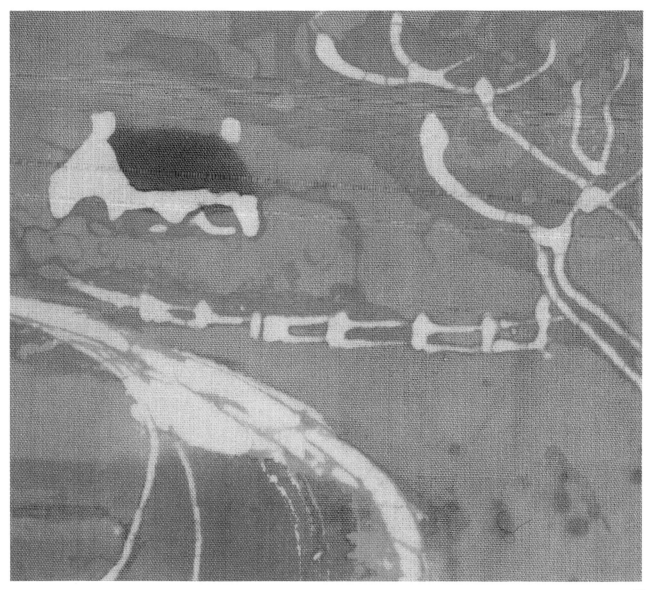

Summer waistcoat

White, turquoise and yellow blend to create a light summery feel. The waxed areas are heavily cracked to heighten this effect and to break up the overall white look, without losing the feeling of freshness.

Materials

Purchased waistcoat pattern
White cotton poplin, as required
Yellow, orange, turquoise dyes
Microcrystalline wax

Method

The pattern pieces are cut out of the cotton material and the lining put to one side. The remaining pieces of cotton are laid separately on to newspaper and areas of yellow and orange dye are painted directly on to the fabric. When dry the pieces of cotton are transferred on to greaseproof paper and using a 5 cm (2 in) wide paint brush, broad semicircular lines are waxed randomly on to the material.

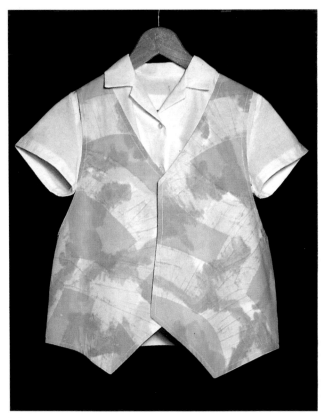

When the wax has cooled, the material is dipped in strong turquoise dye, and the wax is deliberately cracked so that veins of turquoise will appear on the fabric.

The boiling out process is left until the next day and the waistcoat is made up according to the pattern instructions.

Random patterned waistcoat

Beautiful random designs are easily applied using batik. Lovely colours have been used to brighten up this simple waistcoat.

Materials

Purchased waistcoat pattern
White cotton poplin, as required
Red, yellow, blue, black dyes
Microcrystalline wax

Method

Three jars of dye are made up; red, yellow and blue. Two more colours are obtained by combining red and blue to give mauve, and blue and yellow to give green. The pieces of cotton are cut out and the lining pieces are set to one side, as they are to remain white in contrast to the bright colours that are to be applied to the outside of the garment.

The remaining pieces of cotton are laid separately on to sheets of newspaper and random areas of the five colours are painted on, overlapping in some areas and leaving white areas in others.

When dry the pieces of material are placed on greaseproof paper, and an abstract design waxed over the colours. When the wax is cold,

Waistcoat designs by Margaret Hone
Simple waistcoat patterns take on a fresh original look when batik is applied to white cotton. Dyes are painted on to the cut-out pattern pieces, then wax is applied before the final dipping in a dye bath. After the boiling out process, the fabric is allowed to dry and the garments are made up as directed.

it is lightly cracked, by crumpling the batik gently, and the material is laid in a dye bath containing black dye for five minutes.

The boiling out process is left until the next day.

Once the material is completely dry, the waistcoat is made up according to the pattern instructions. The final result is a brightly coloured garment with a contrasting white lining.

Summer shirts for men

The two shirts shown here illustrate how batik can transform ordinary white cotton shirts into striking designs, using bold, vibrant colours. Both 'painting-on' and the dipping of dyes are used to create the colours and patterns, which are planned from sketches and photographs.

Materials

2 purchased white cotton shirts
Paraffin wax
'Jungle' shirt: yellow, red, turquoise, brilliant blue, royal blue dyes
'Sailboard' shirt: yellow, turquoise, royal blue, brilliant red dyes

Method

The designs are drawn, or traced, on to the shirts. During the waxing and dyeing process, the fronts and backs of the shirts are worked separately. Each section is spread out flat – on greaseproof paper while waxing, and on newspaper while painting. Greaseproof paper is inserted into the sleeves.

'Jungle' shirt: hot wax is applied over the areas to remain white, on the single thickness of fabric, using a tjanting and brushes.
The shirt is then spread out on newspaper and yellow and red dyes randomly painted on, allowing the colours to merge in places. Water and a weak solution of turquoise dye are brushed on between the red and yellow areas. Care is taken to apply the colours to the back of the sleeves. Areas of red and yellow are retained by waxing and leaf shapes are waxed on to the fabric.
When dry, more leaf and tree shapes are waxed on to the fabric and the palm tree trunks cracked by pinching the waxed cloth. The shirt is then dipped in brilliant blue dye.
When dry, more shapes are waxed on and the final dipping is in royal blue dye.
When dry, the wax is boiled out.

Shirt designs by Heather Griffin
A holiday wardrobe can be livened up by applying dyes and wax to ready-made white cotton shirts. Here, the jungle and a seascape offer inspiration for two colourful designs.

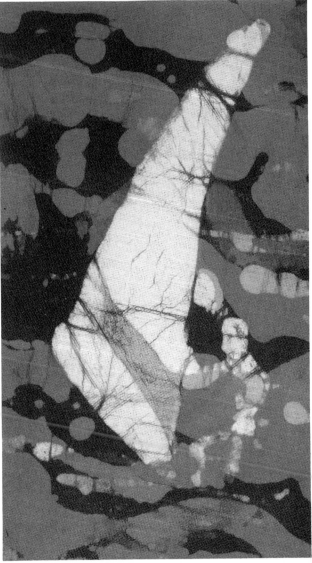

'Sailboard' shirt: The same method of painting, waxing and dyeing is used. The sailboard outlines are waxed, then green (turquoise and yellow) is painted on some sails. The green areas are waxed and the shirt is dipped in turquoise dye.

The turquoise is then waxed in some areas and the shirt dipped in blue dye.

The shirt is then waxed through the double thickness of fabric to create the impression of waves, before finally dipping it in brilliant red dye.

When dry the wax is boiled out.

Landscape shirt

The batik design on this shirt was freely adapted from sketches and photographs, to give the impression of a landscape. The blue on the collar represents sky and a stream meanders round the hips, separating green fields from wooded slopes. When creating a design like this, always expect the unexpected! The original design constantly changes throughout the waxing and dyeing processes as colours mix and blend. Follow the guidelines below to create your own unique design.

Materials

Ready-made purchased long-sleeved baggy shirt in white cotton
Turquoise, yellow, brilliant blue, royal blue, brilliant red dyes
Paraffin wax

Method

The buttons are removed and pencil guidelines indicating the position of cottages, fields and the skyline are drawn on to the shirt.

The shirt is laid out flat on a sheet of greaseproof paper in preparation for waxing. It is waxed from the front, through the double thickness, giving the same design in reverse on the back. First all the areas to remain white are waxed i.e clouds, cottage walls, fences and flowers.

As the next stage is painting the dye on to the fabric, the shirt is transferred on to newspaper (or absorbent paper) and the colours applied through the double thickness. Yellow and a weak mix of brilliant blue are made up and applied to the material using large brushes. The yellow is painted on to represent fields and the blue to represent sky (on the

collar) and the stream. With a small brush a weak mix of brilliant red is painted on to the cottage roofs.

Check the back of the shirt to make sure the colours have penetrated the double thickness and retouch any areas that need colour. Colours may spread or blend on the fabric. Don't worry, these can be adapted as part of the landscape as the dyeing process continues!

When dry, the shirt is once more transferred on to a sheet of greaseproof paper. Wax is applied over the yellow fields, the blue sky and stream, and the cottage roofs. Areas where the blue and yellow dyes have merged to create green, are waxed into tree shapes.

The shirt is then dipped in the turquoise dye. When dry, wax is again applied over certain areas of the turquoise. This creates turquoise trees, a wooded skyline, a turquoise cottage roof and flowers and grasses.

The shirt is then dipped in yellow dye. The unwaxed turquoise areas blend with the yellow dye to give green.

When dry, wax is applied to the fields, and some trees and hedges. The final dipping is in royal blue dye.

The wax is boiled out. Several boilings are needed and care must be taken to squeeze out the collar and cuffs so that hard lumps of wax do not collect in the double thicknesses and seams when the shirt is plunged into cold water. Rinse the shirt in cold water each time after boiling.

Shirt design by Heather Griffin
This landscape design is gradually built up by freehand waxing and dyeing. Areas are waxed on to the plain white fabric to represent clouds, cottages, fences and flowers, and yellows and blues merge and mix to give green fields, hedges and trees. The picture on the right shows a detail of the finished design.

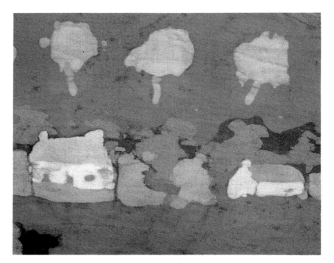

Summer coat

Vibrant colours transform a simple shirt into a lovely summer coat. A purchased shirt pattern is used, but the garment is cut longer than the original design by extending the pattern guide-lines and extra large pockets are added as a special feature. The design is simplified by omitting buttons and buttonholes, and no frame is used when waxing and dyeing because of the large size of the pieces of fabric.

Materials

Purchased pattern
White cotton poplin as required
Pale blue, red, yellow dyes
Microcrystalline wax

Method

Large pieces of material are difficult to handle when wet, so the fabric is cut into two smaller pieces. The best way to do this is to lay the pattern pieces on to the material before deciding where to cut (remembering to remove the pattern pieces before commencing).

Lay the material on to clean dry newspaper and using a small brush paint on random areas of pale blue, pale red and yellow. When dry, transfer the pieces of material to large *flat* sheets of plastic. Large squares are waxed on to the dyed fabric using a 5cm (2in) brush. As the wax cools, the plastic will easily peel away. (A small amount of wax will be left on the plastic, so check the back of the fabric to see whether any re-waxing is required). The material is now dipped in a bright red/pink dye. Some red cracks will appear in the waxed areas at this stage.

After it has been hung out to dry, the material is again spread out on to plastic and re-waxed; lines are drawn in wax round the already waxed squared, making larger squares. In some areas the red cracks are re-waxed to prevent the next colour from penetrating them, but many are left.

The fabric is removed, as before, and placed in a fresh dye bath containing yellow dye. Again new cracks are made in the wax and now there are red and yellow cracks – and orange where the two colours have combined.

The wax is removed the next day, when the fabric is completely dry. After the final washing and ironing, cut out the pattern pieces and make up the garment as directed.

Coat design by Margaret Hone
A purchased shirt pattern is used to make a colourful summer coat. Red, yellow and blue dyes combine to create a lovely batik design.

Simple cotton coat

This simple design has no collar or buttons and it makes good use of lovely bold, contrasting colours. The material was found in a market and it was a real bargain! Useful material can often be found in markets, but be sure that any you buy for batik is pure cotton and not a synthetic fibre. The cotton used for this coat had to be washed thoroughly to soften it.

Materials

Purchased pattern
White cotton as required
Pale blue, yellow, red, orange, navy, black dyes
Microcrystalline wax

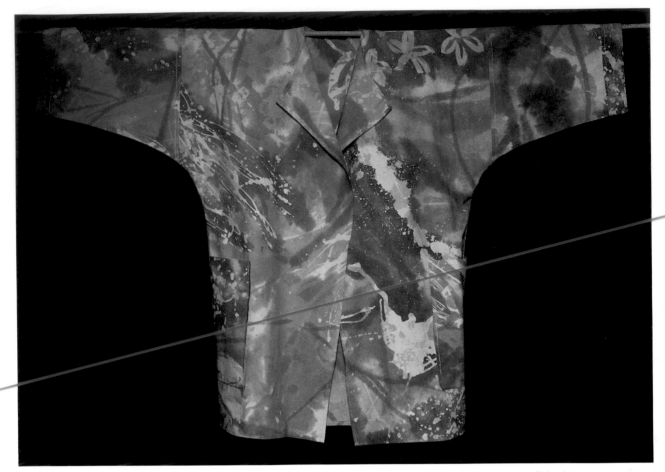

Simple cotton coat by Margaret Hone

Method

Before commencing, cut the material into manageable lengths, after the pattern pieces have been placed upon it for guidance. Dye these lengths in pale blue dye and hang them up to dry.

Transfer the material on to clean dry newspaper and paint on several lines of black dye. Allow to dry and then transfer the material to a frame and wax abstract leaf shapes over the surface using a small brush.

Lovely effects can be achieved at this stage by allowing the wax to drip haphazardly from the brush while tipping the frame up slightly. This encourages the wax to flow freely.

When the wax is dry, place plenty of newspapers under the frame and randomly paint on yellow, red, orange and navy dyes. Allow the

44

dyes to overlap in some places to give different colours.

When the material is dry, remove the wax. After the final washing and ironing, cut out the pattern pieces and make up the garment as directed.

Summer coats

Pretty flower and leaf designs are applied in wax over random-dyed cotton poplin (above) and cotton lawn (below). These two coats illustrate the simple use of batik on large pieces of material, as there is only one waxing session on each garment.

Materials

2 purchased patterns
Microcrystalline wax
Random patterned coat (above) : white cotton poplin as required; red, blue, yellow dyes
Summer flower coat (below) : fine white cotton lawn as required; blue, yellow, green, tan dyes

Method for random patterned coat

Spread the material out on clean, dry newspaper and paint on random areas of red, blue and yellow, leaving some white spaces between the coloured areas. When the dyes are dry, transfer the material on to flat sheets of plastic and wax flower and leaf shapes over the whole surface.

Remove the material from the plastic sheets and transfer on to clean newspaper; apply red, yellow and blue dyes to the unwaxed areas in a random fashion. Leave the material to dry overnight and remove the wax the next day. After washing and ironing, cut out the pattern pieces and make up the garment as directed.

Method for summer flower coat

This coat is designed to retain much of the basic white of the cotton to give a fresh look. The material is cut into workable sections and a few random patches of pale red and blue are applied with a 2.5 cm (1 in) brush, after the material has been spread out on fresh dry newspaper. As only a small amount of the dye is used, the material is so fine it dries quickly on the absorbent paper. After transferring the material on to a sheet of plastic, a simple flower design is waxed freely over the surface.

Transfer the material on to clean, dry newspaper and paint yellow and tan dyes on to a few of the unwaxed areas that are now enclosed with wax. As very little colour is being added to the fabric each time, there is no need to dip the garment into the dye bath.

The wax is removed when the material is completely dry. After the final washing and ironing, cut out the pattern pieces and make up the garment as directed.

Random patterned coat by Margaret Hone

Summer flower coat by Margaret Hone

The Hollyford Track

This picture is based on a photograph of the Hollyford Track, a path which runs through the bush in New Zealand's South Island. It shows a much more involved use of colour and composition than the other projects, and is therefore not suitable for a beginner. However, it is an example of what can be achieved with patience and perseverance.

Materials

69 × 81 cm (27 × 32 in) white cotton, noting that 5 cm (2 in) is allowed all round for glueing the edges of the picture, giving a finished size of 63 × 76 cm (25 × 30 in)

Yellow, orange, red, brown, olive green, light and dark blue dyes

Paraffin wax

Method

The picture is worked on a frame. Pencil guidelines are made on the cotton, to indicate the main areas of light, and the shape of the path.

Wax is applied using a tjanting and a fine brush, to areas to be kept very light – tops of ferns, foliage and the light between trees.

Different strengths of yellow and orange dyes are painted on, using the photograph as reference, and water is brushed on to weaken the dye in the lightest areas.

Areas between the trees, branches and foliage are kept in wax, using the tjanting and a fine brush. Painting continues in this way, using red and a weak blue dye to create some greens and browns. Small sections are waxed, to retain varying colours and shapes.

The main shape of the distant light area is waxed, and the path, also green areas amongst the trees.

Red, green and brown dyes are freely painted on and waxed until the completed batik is covered in wax. This is then cracked by crushing and pinching the material to form patterns in the wax so creating the effect of foliage. It is then dipped in dark green dye.

When dry, the wax is boiled out so that the progression of colours can be checked. At this stage the design can be altered, or any shapes that are too light, changed. Areas that are to be retained are then rewaxed, some shapes altered and some new ones made. The line of the cracking can be followed with the wax, creating interesting branch shapes. The painting on of dyes and the waxing continue as before.

The darkest of the tree trunks are kept free of wax until the final dipping in dark blue which gives a dark brown. The waxed cotton is crumpled and folded to give some dark cracking, so adding to the impression of light and shade in the forest.

When dry, the wax is boiled out and the finished picture again allowed to dry.

To Complete

The following techniques for framing a batik may be used for both cotton and silk, but it may be advisable to cover a silk painting with glass for protection.

You may decide to make your own frame and in this event, a natural wooden frame is most effective and inexpensive. A professional picture framer could also mount and frame your batik, if you prefer.

A batik picture can be stretched over a piece of hardboard before it is framed. When calculating the size of the hardboard, allow at least 5 cm (2 in) *less* all round than the finished size of the fabric, so that the cloth can be overlapped all round and glued to the back of the board.

Paint the *smooth* side of the hardboard with white emulsion paint to give the best results. Allow to dry. Now stretch the batik firmly over the white painted side of the board, glue securely to the back with adhesive, and neaten the edges with masking tape.

Allow the mount to dry thoroughly before framing the picture.

The Hollyford Track by Heather Griffin

46

First published in Great Britain 1989 by
Search Press Ltd.
Wellwood, North Farm Road
Tunbridge Wells
Kent TN2 3DR

Reprinted 1998, 2000, 2001, 2002, 2004

ISBN 0 85532 619 0

Typeset by Scribe Design, Gillingham, Kent.
Printed by Times Offset (M) Sdn. Bhd., Malaysia